WE DIG WORMS!

A TOON BOOK BY
KEVIN McCLOSKEY

For my wife, Mama Patt,
who asked for a fun worm book to read at the library.

THERE ARE MANY DIFFERENT WORMS.

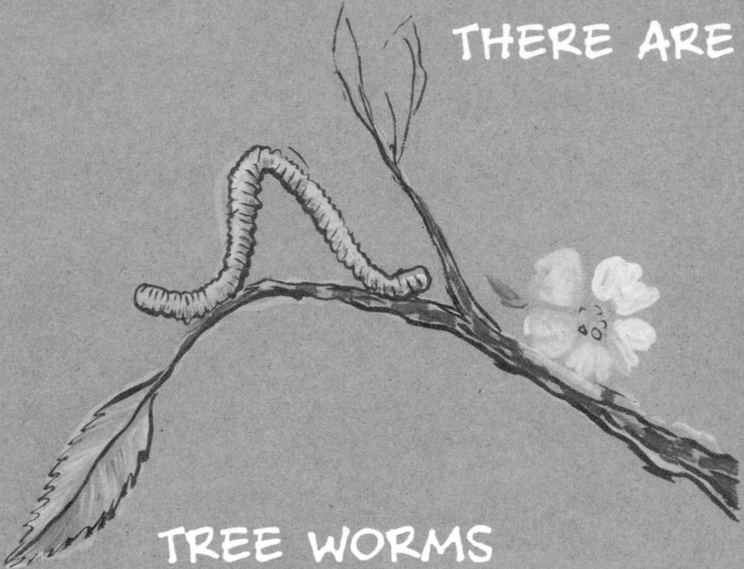

TREE WORMS

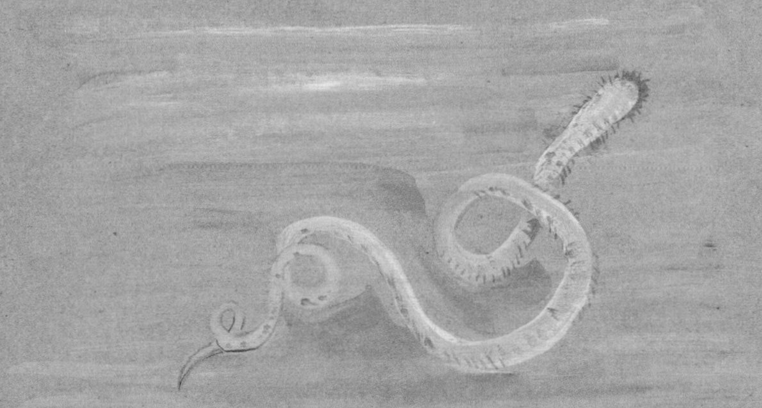

SEA WORMS

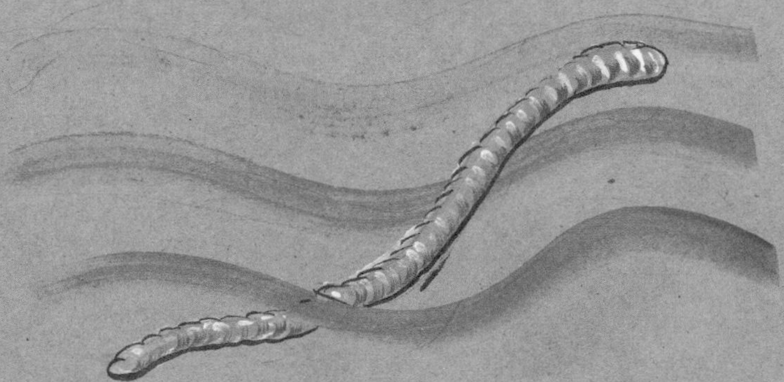

RIVER WORMS

...AND GUMMMY WORMS!

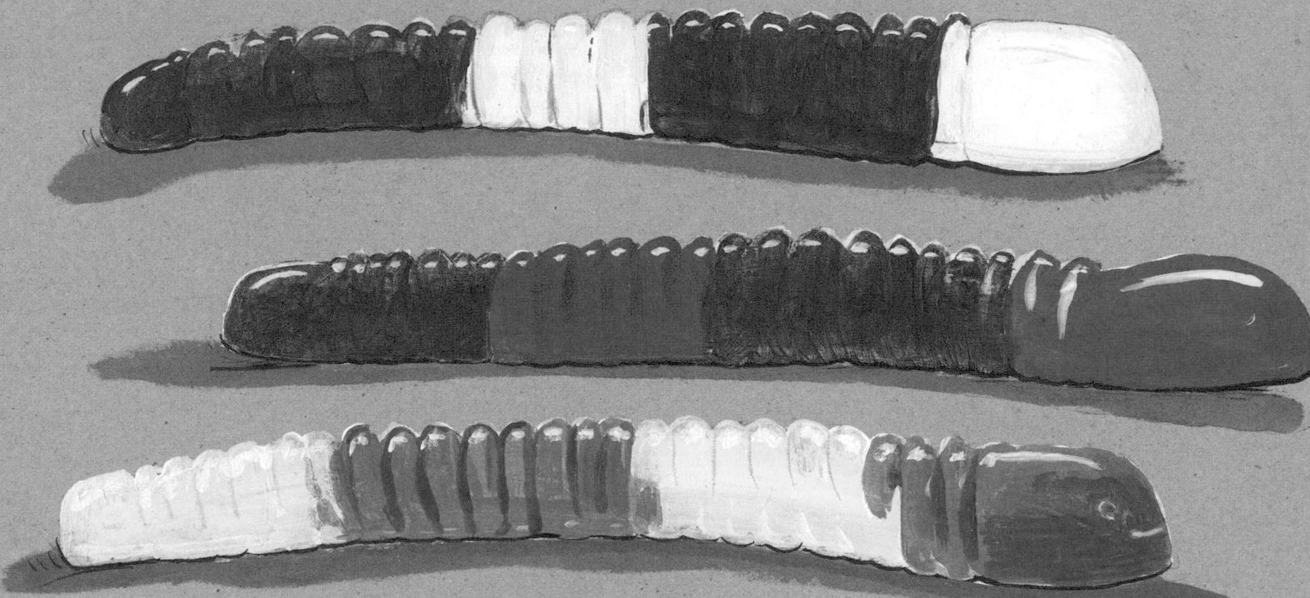

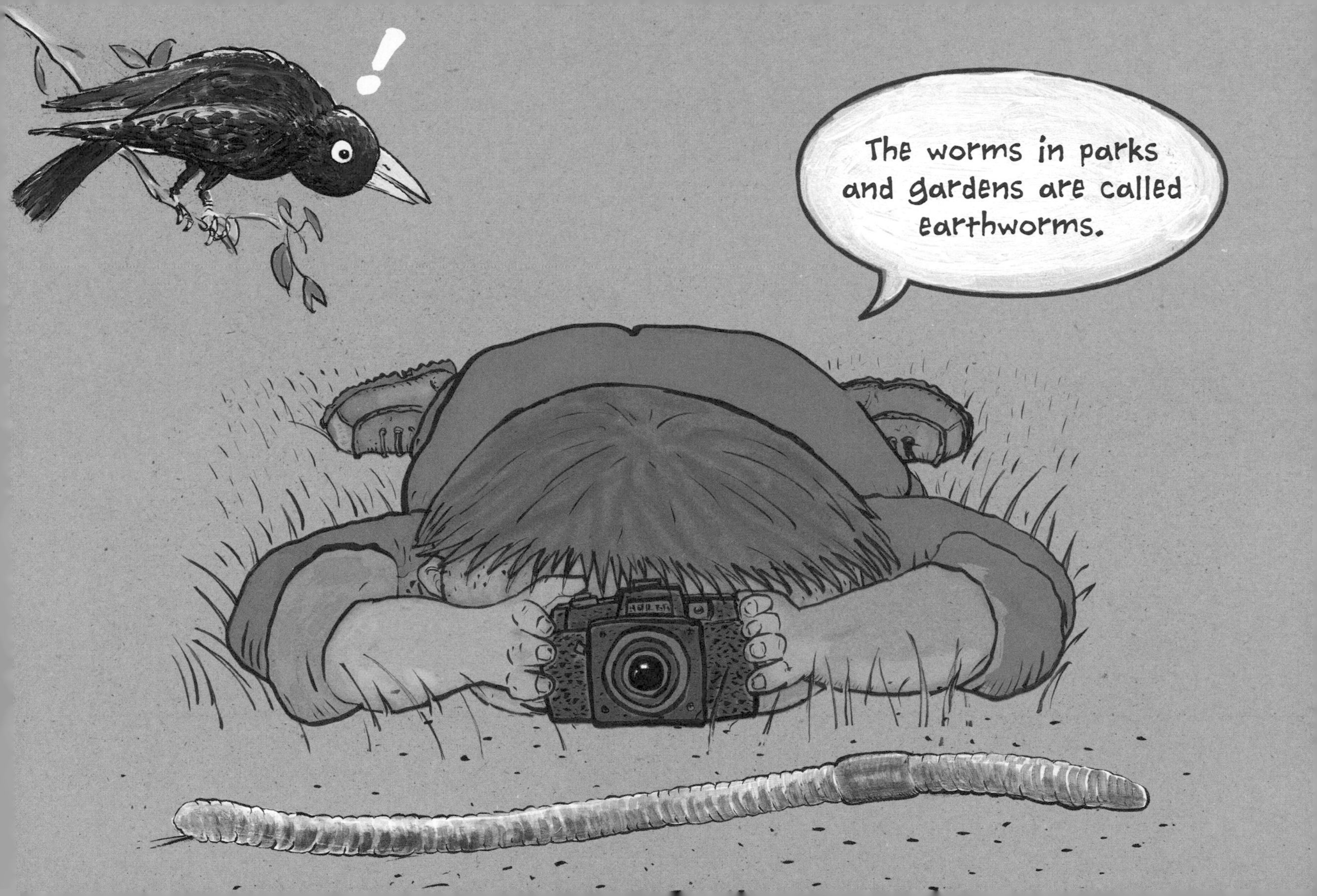
The worms in parks and gardens are called earthworms.

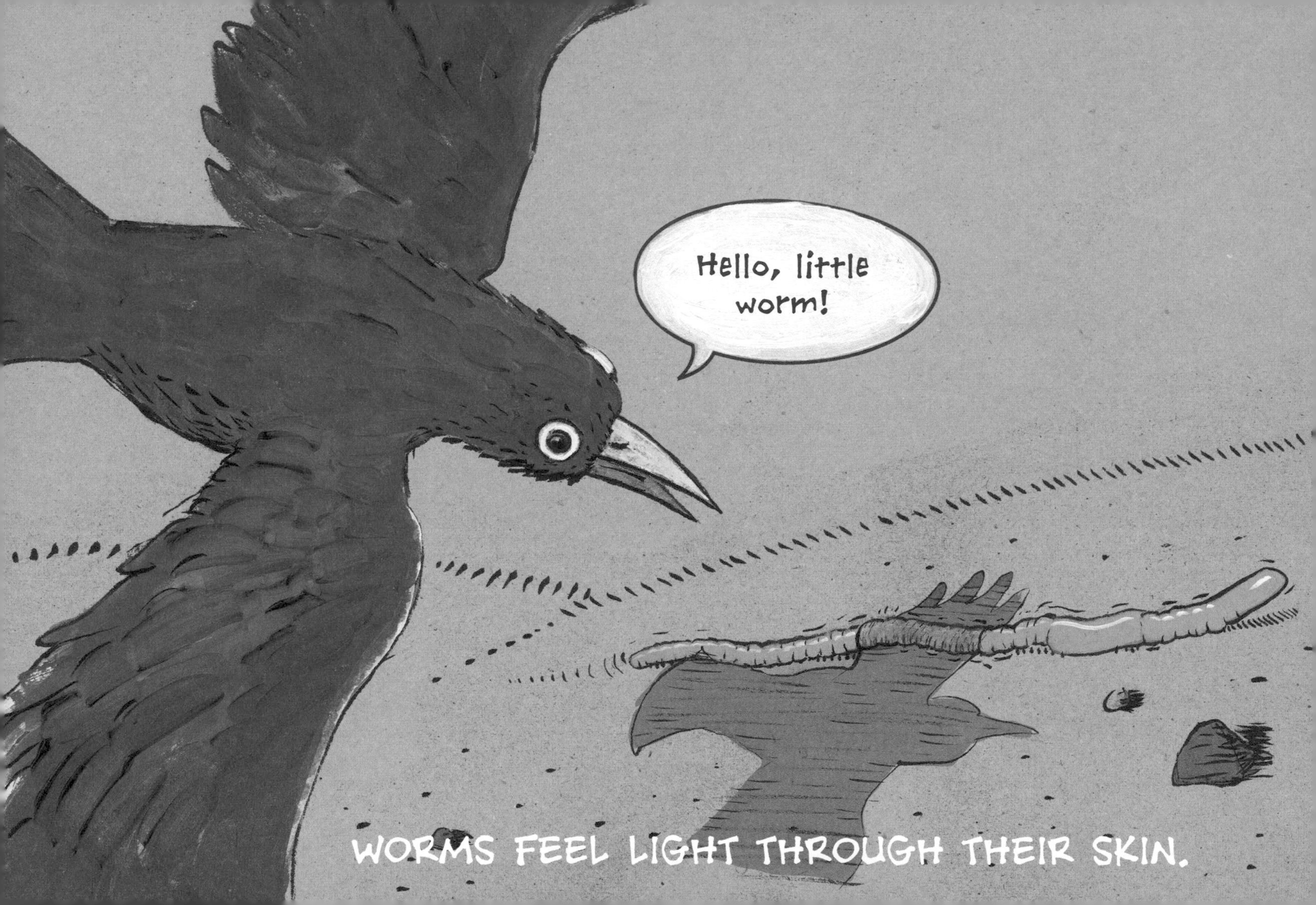
Hello, little worm!
WORMS FEEL LIGHT THROUGH THEIR SKIN.

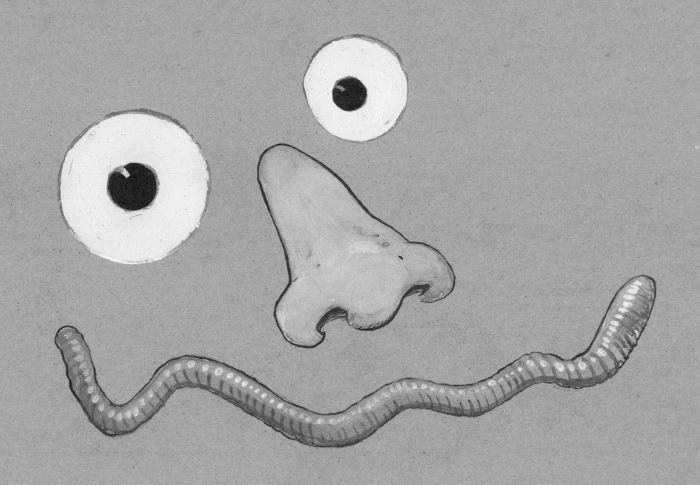

THEY HAVE NO **EYES** AND NO **NOSE**.

WORMS DO A LOT OF IMPORTANT WORK.

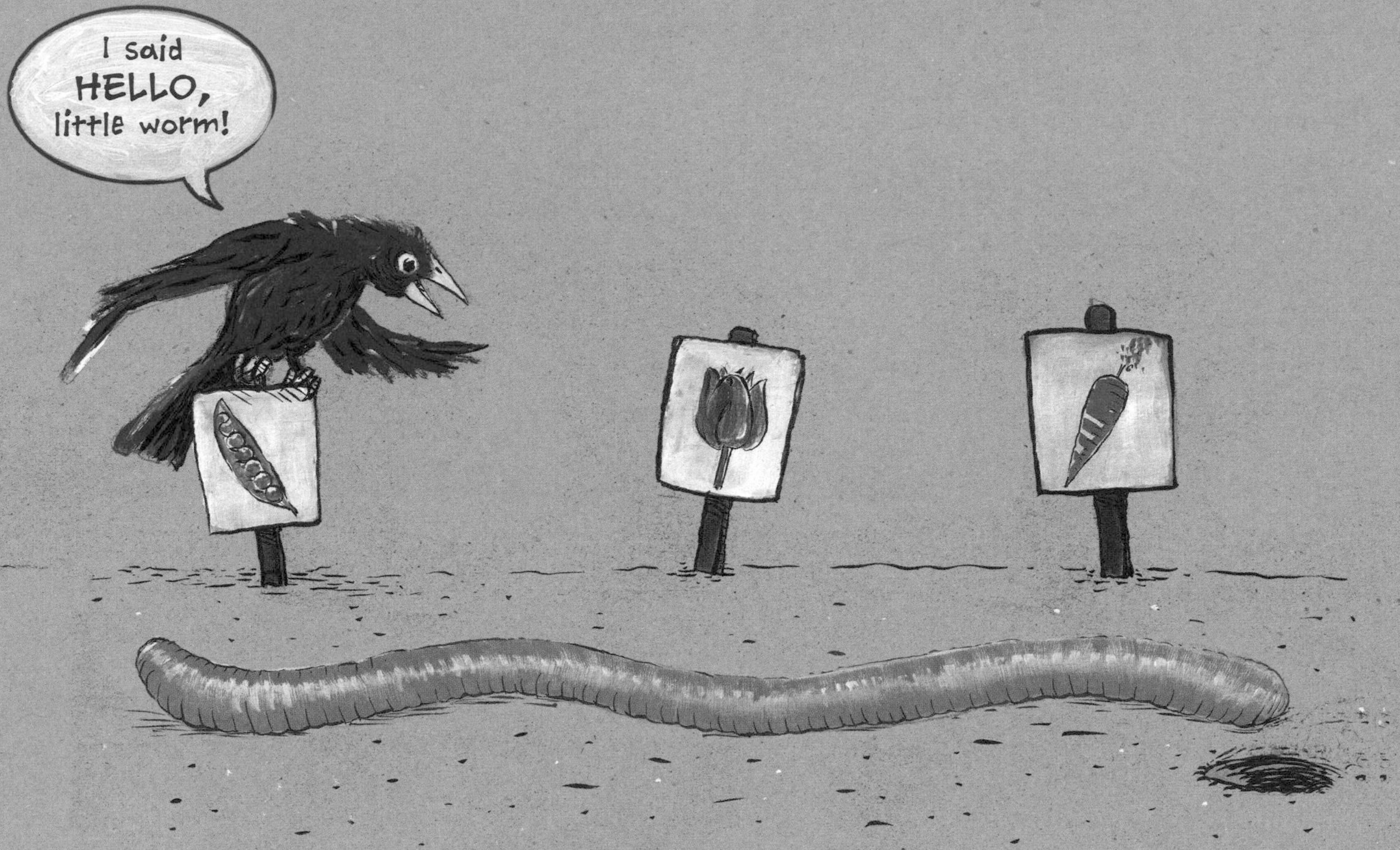
I said HELLO, little worm!

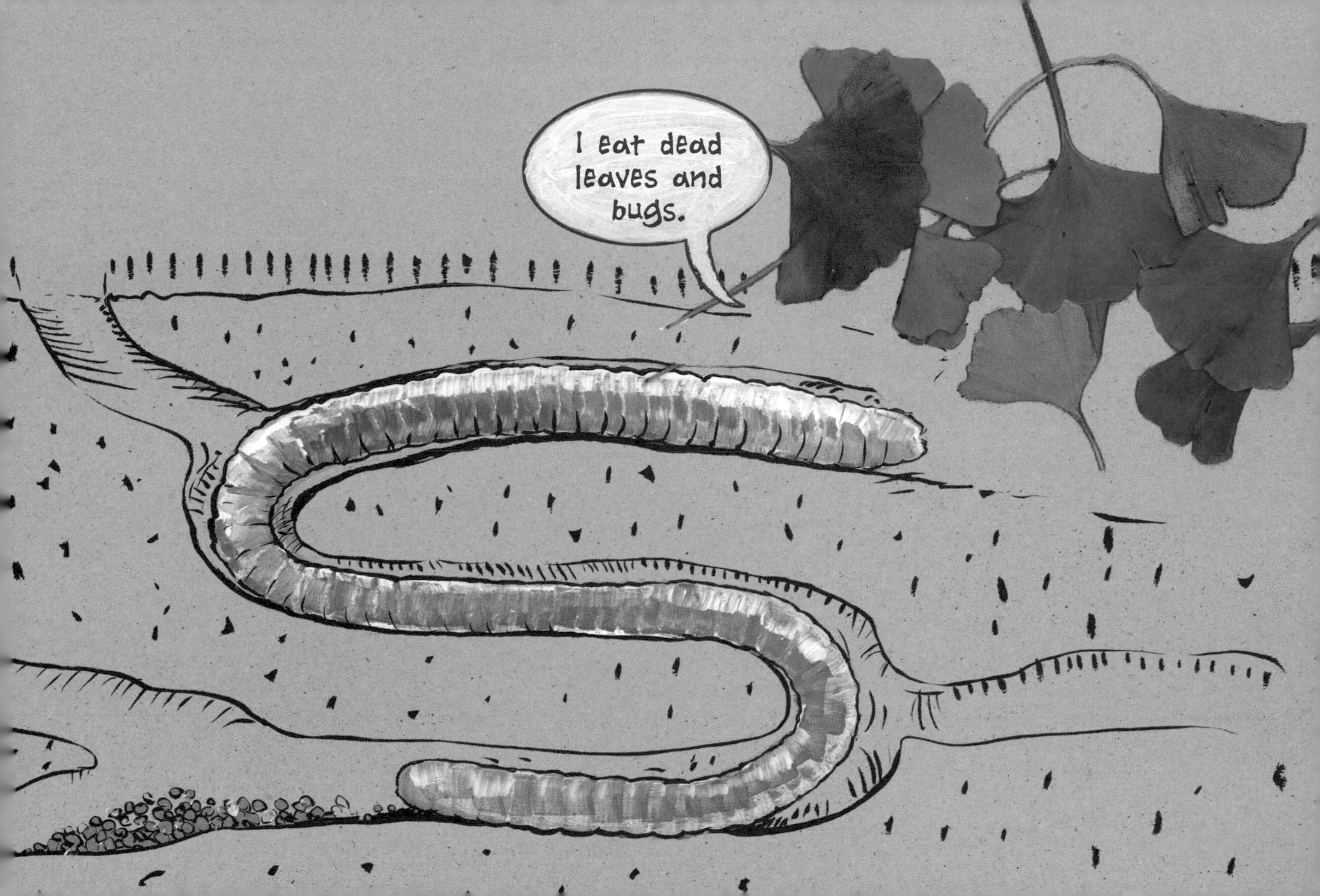
I eat dead leaves and bugs.

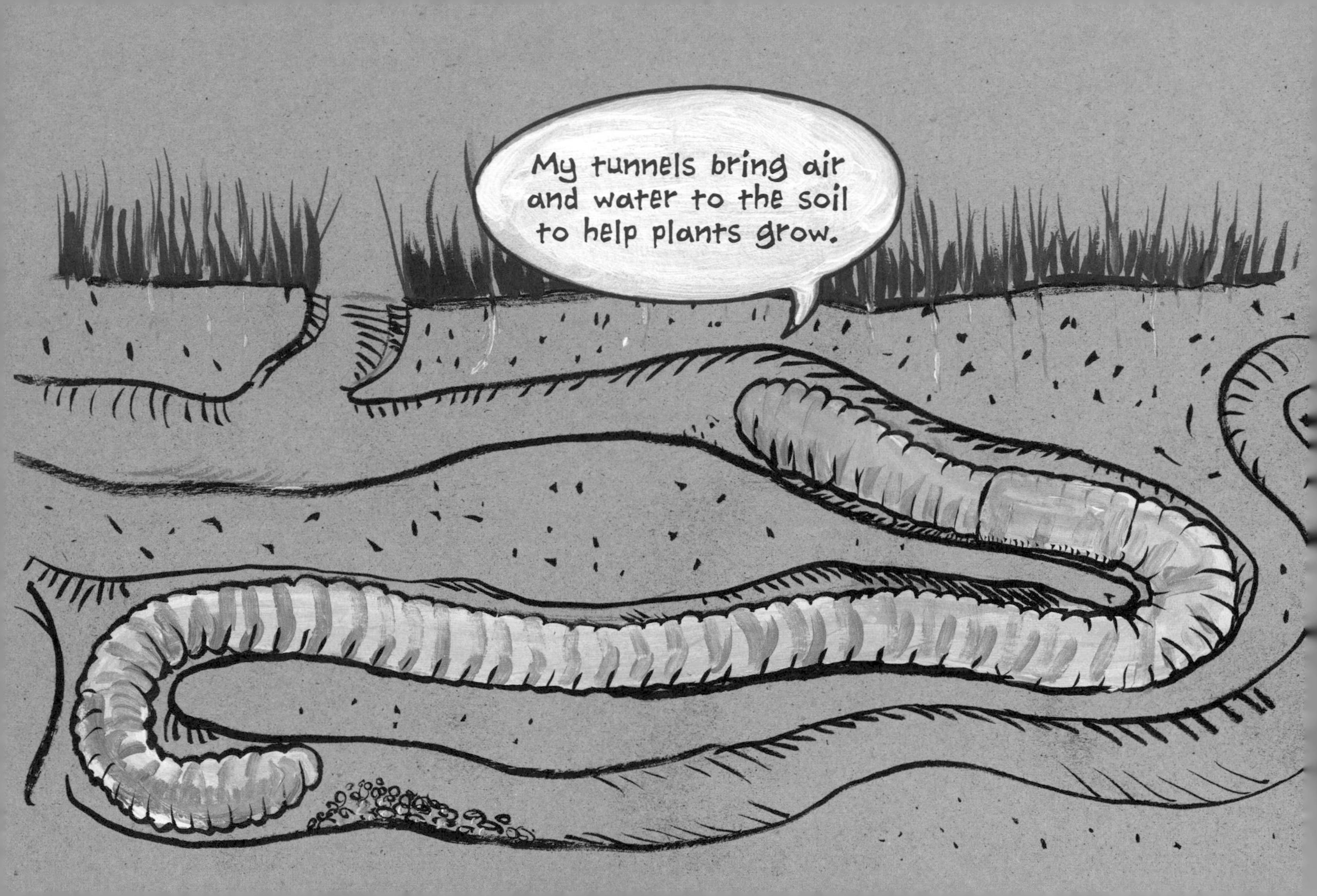
My tunnels bring air and water to the soil to help plants grow.

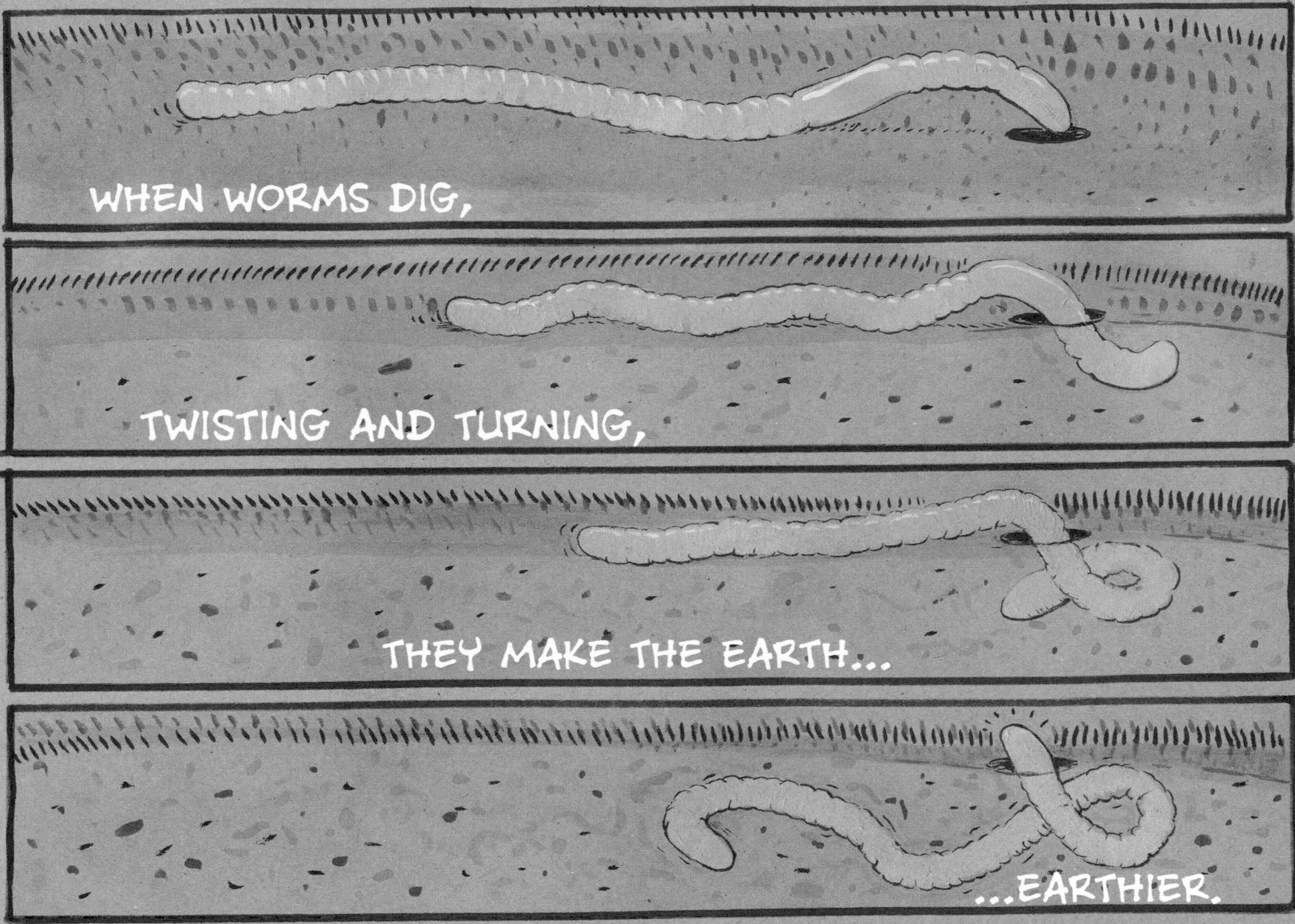
WHEN WORMS DIG,
TWISTING AND TURNING,
THEY MAKE THE EARTH...
...EARTHIER.

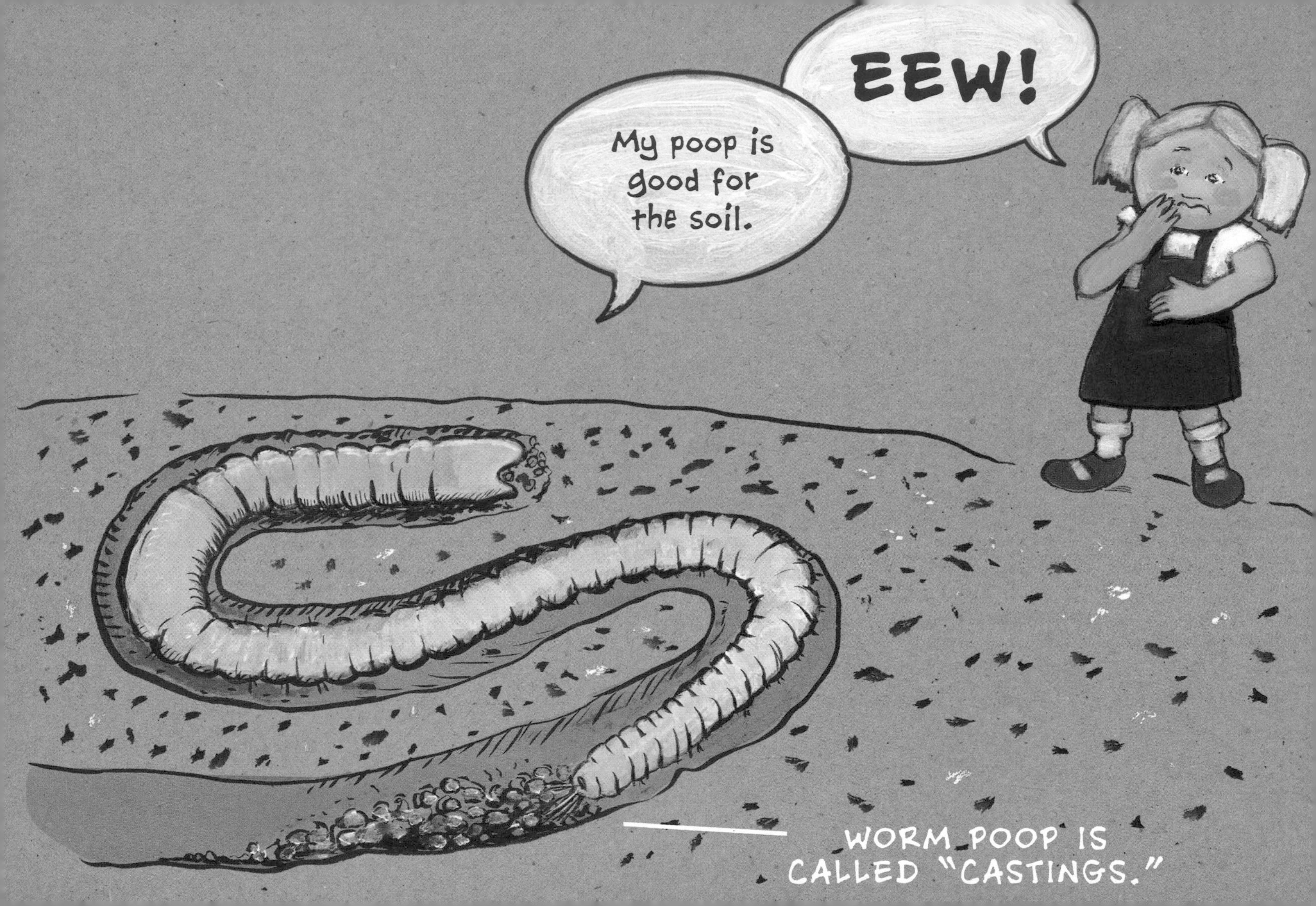
My poop is good for the soil.
EEW!
WORM POOP IS CALLED "CASTINGS."

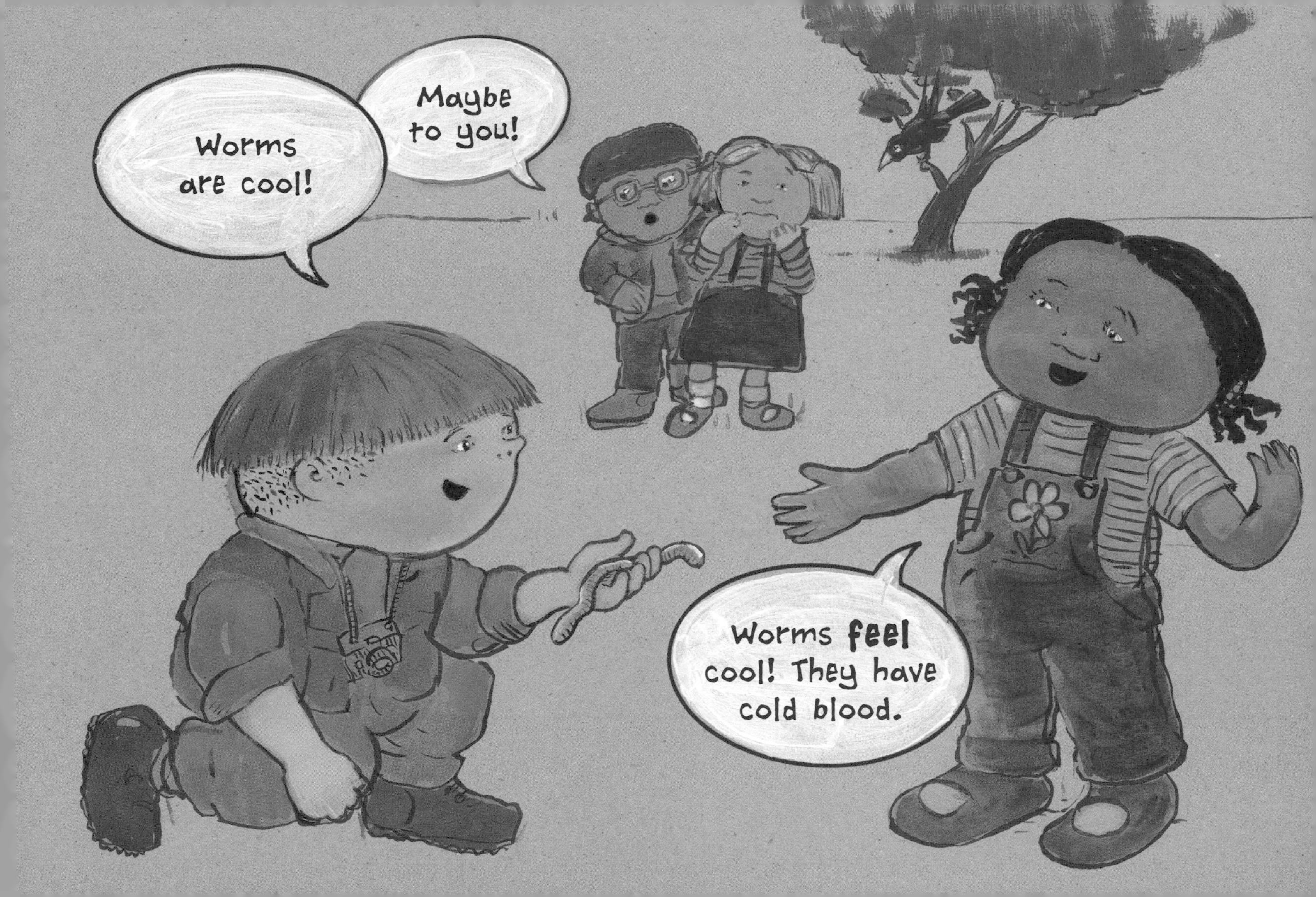
Worms are cool!
Maybe to you!
Worms **feel** cool! They have cold blood.

COCOONS

Worms are born from cocoons.

SETAE

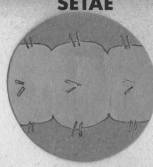

Setae are tiny bristles that help worms move.

OUTSIDE:

Worms don't have lungs. They breathe through their skin.

INSIDE:

Only muscles & nerves. Worms have no bones.

ANUS　　　**INTESTINE**

MAP OF THE WORM

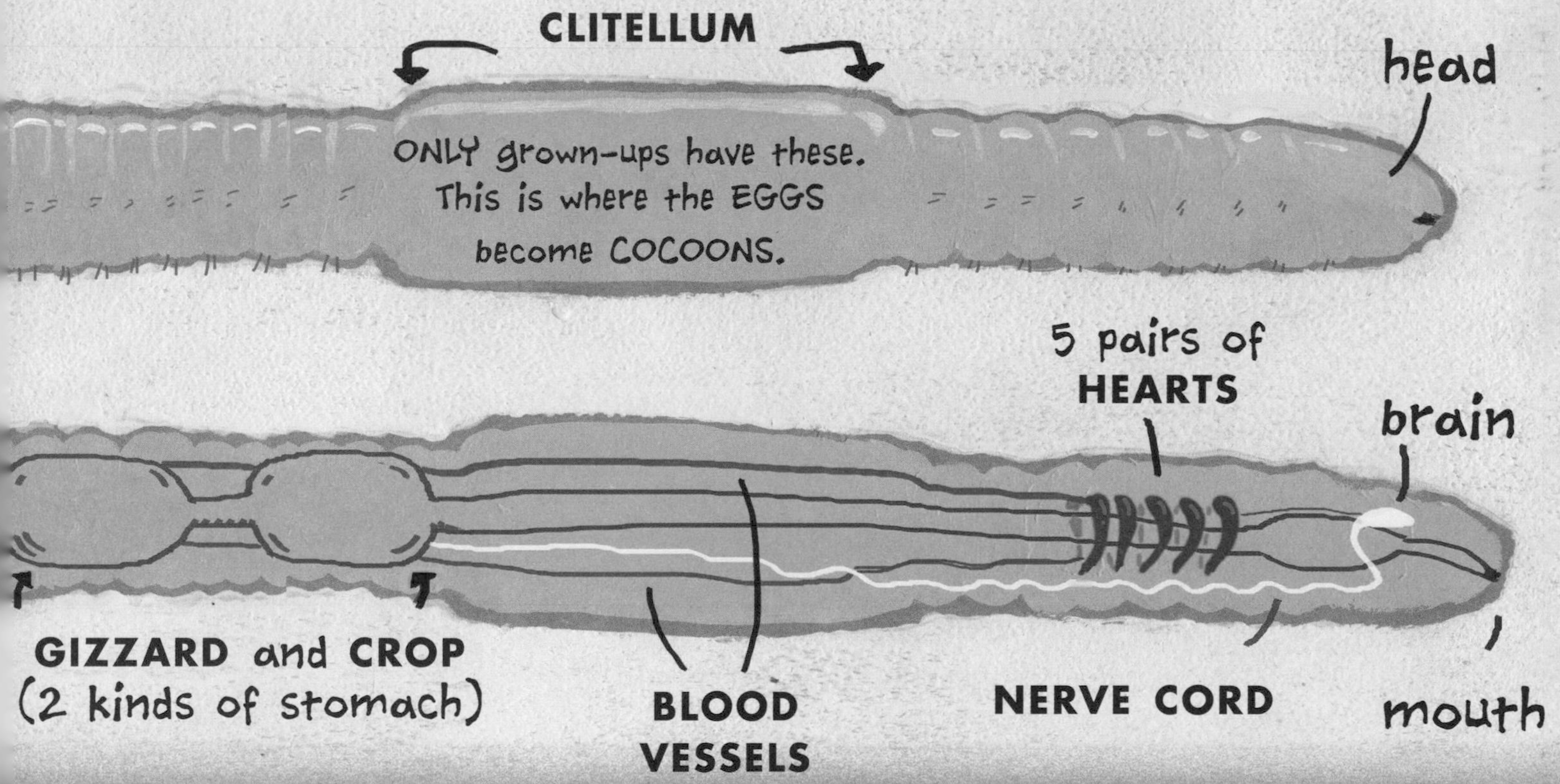

CLITELLUM
head
ONLY grown-ups have these.
This is where the EGGS
become COCOONS.
5 pairs of
HEARTS
brain
GIZZARD and CROP
(2 kinds of stomach)
BLOOD
VESSELS
NERVE CORD
mouth

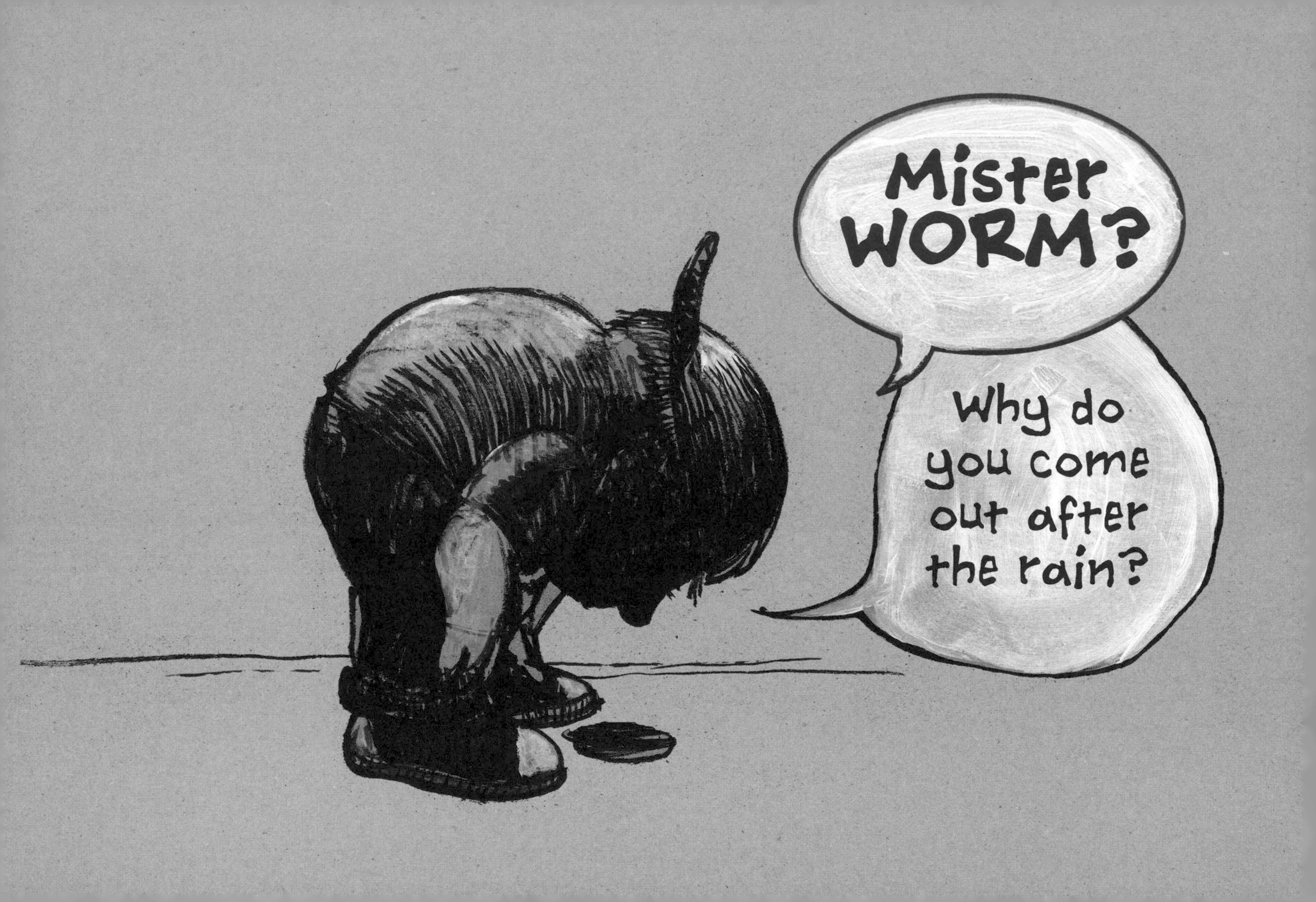
Mister WORM?
Why do you come out after the rain?

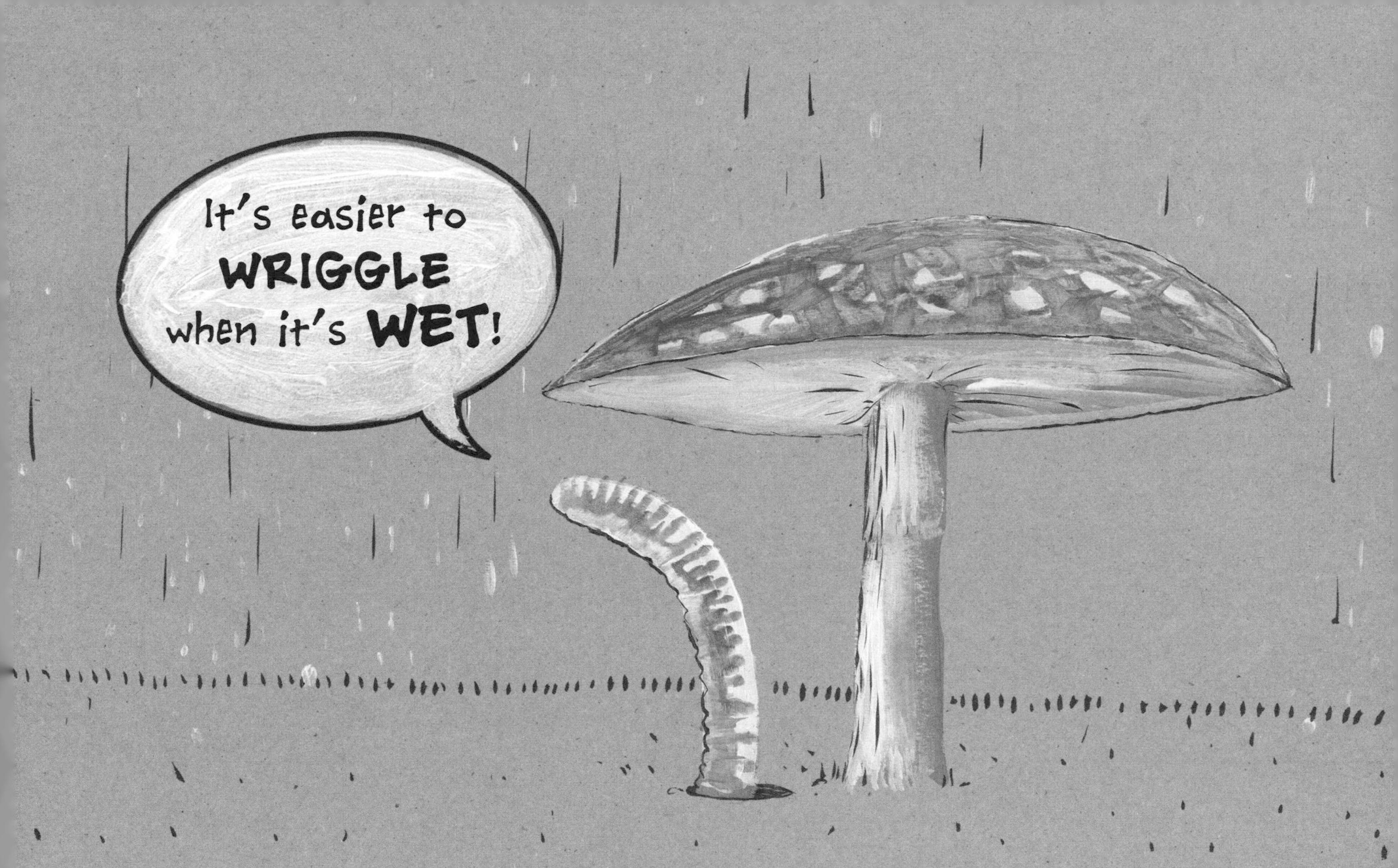
It's easier to WRIGGLE when it's WET!

WORMS MOVE AND BREATHE BETTER WHEN IT'S WET.

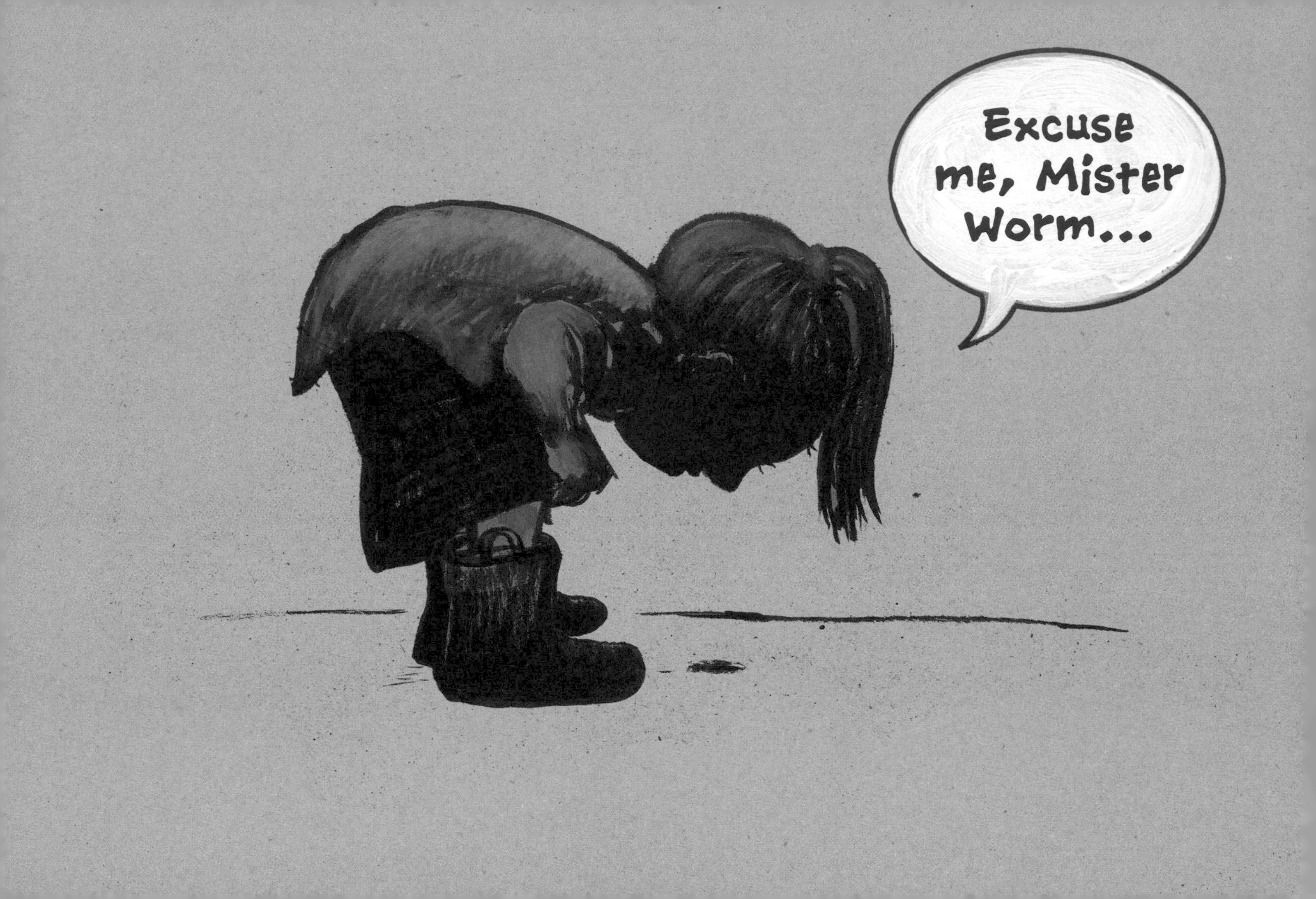
Excuse me, Mister Worm...

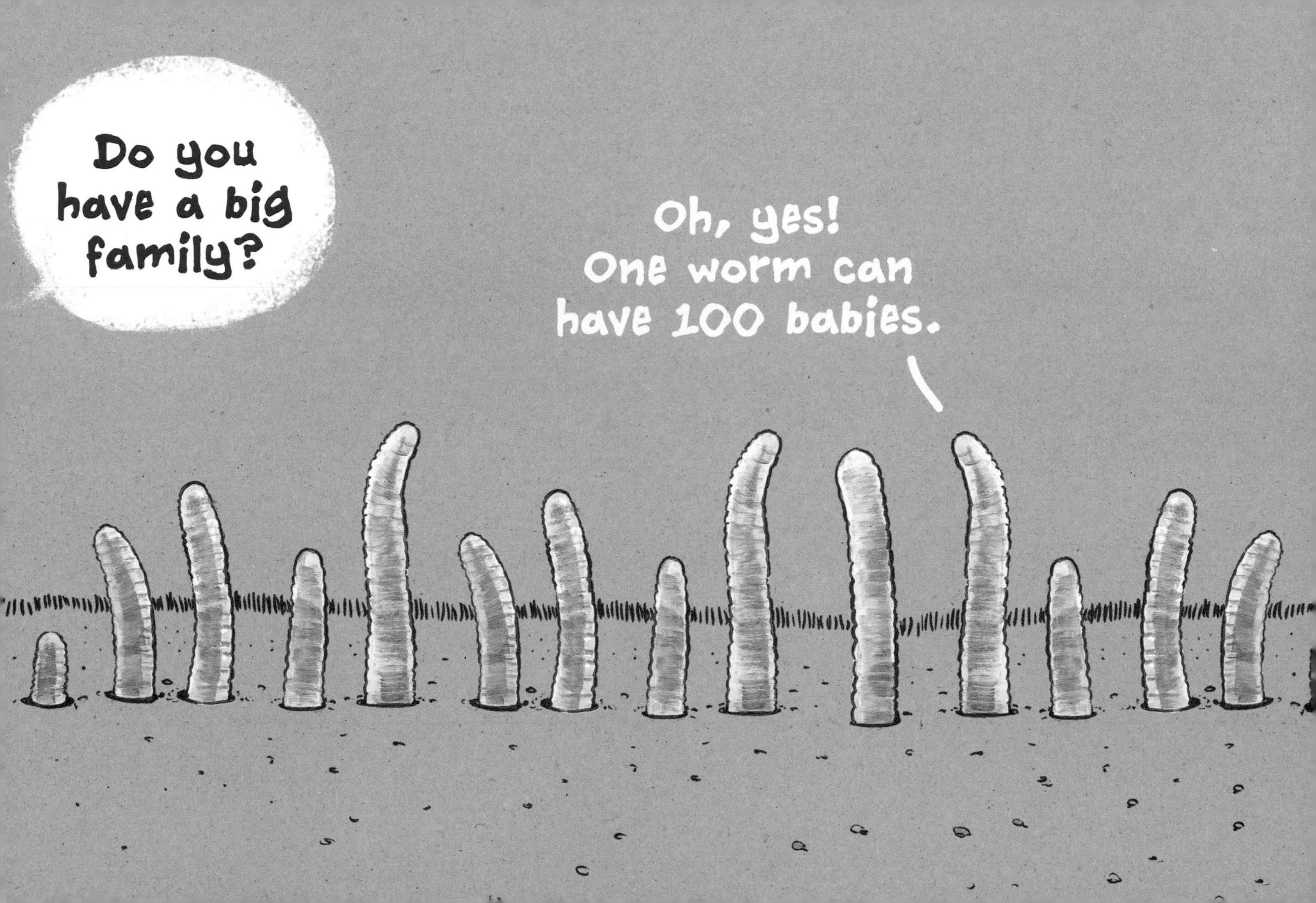
Do you have a big family?
Oh, yes! One worm can have 100 babies.

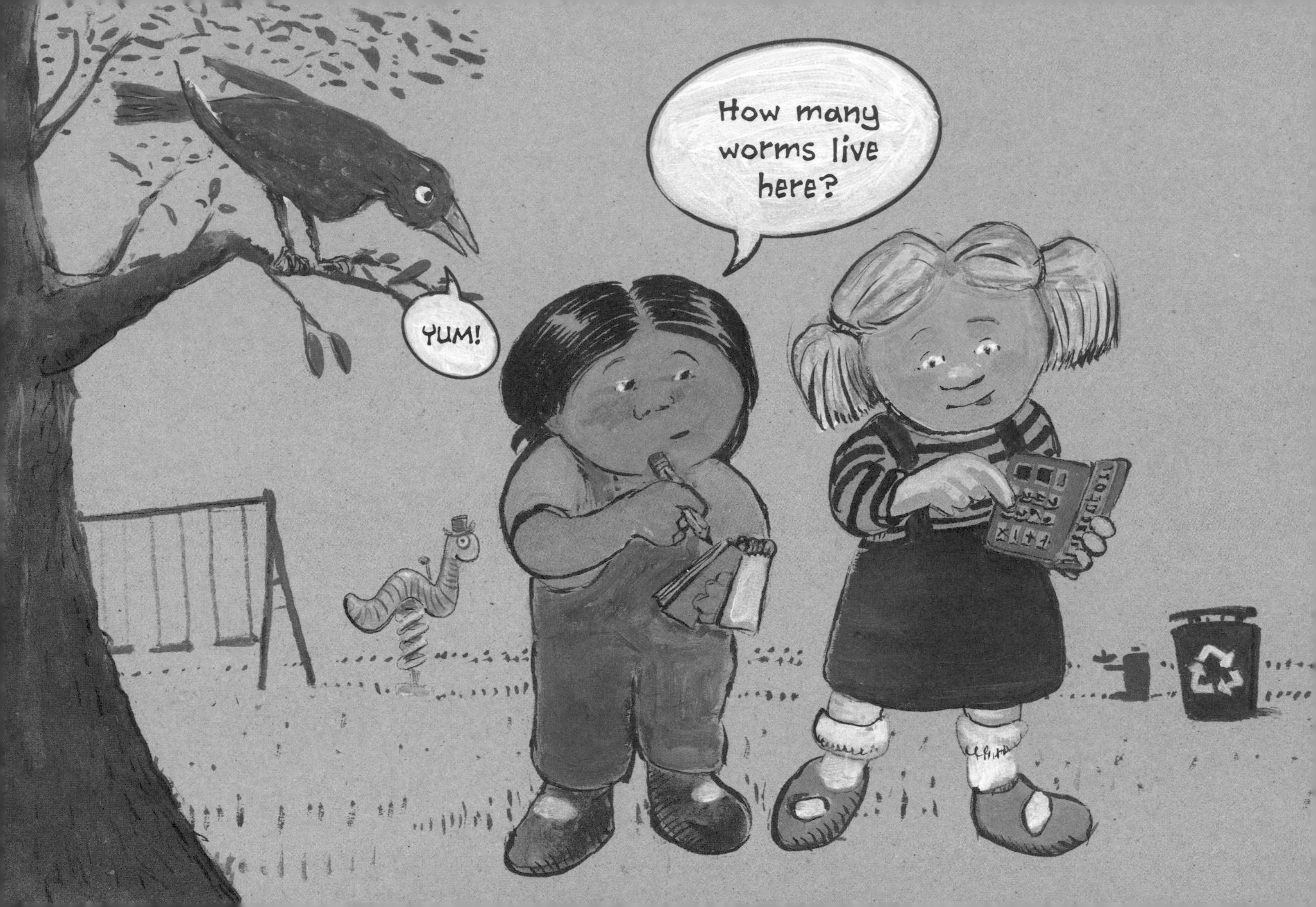
YUM!
How many worms live here?

Millions! Millions! Millions! Millions! Millions! Millions! Millions! Millions!

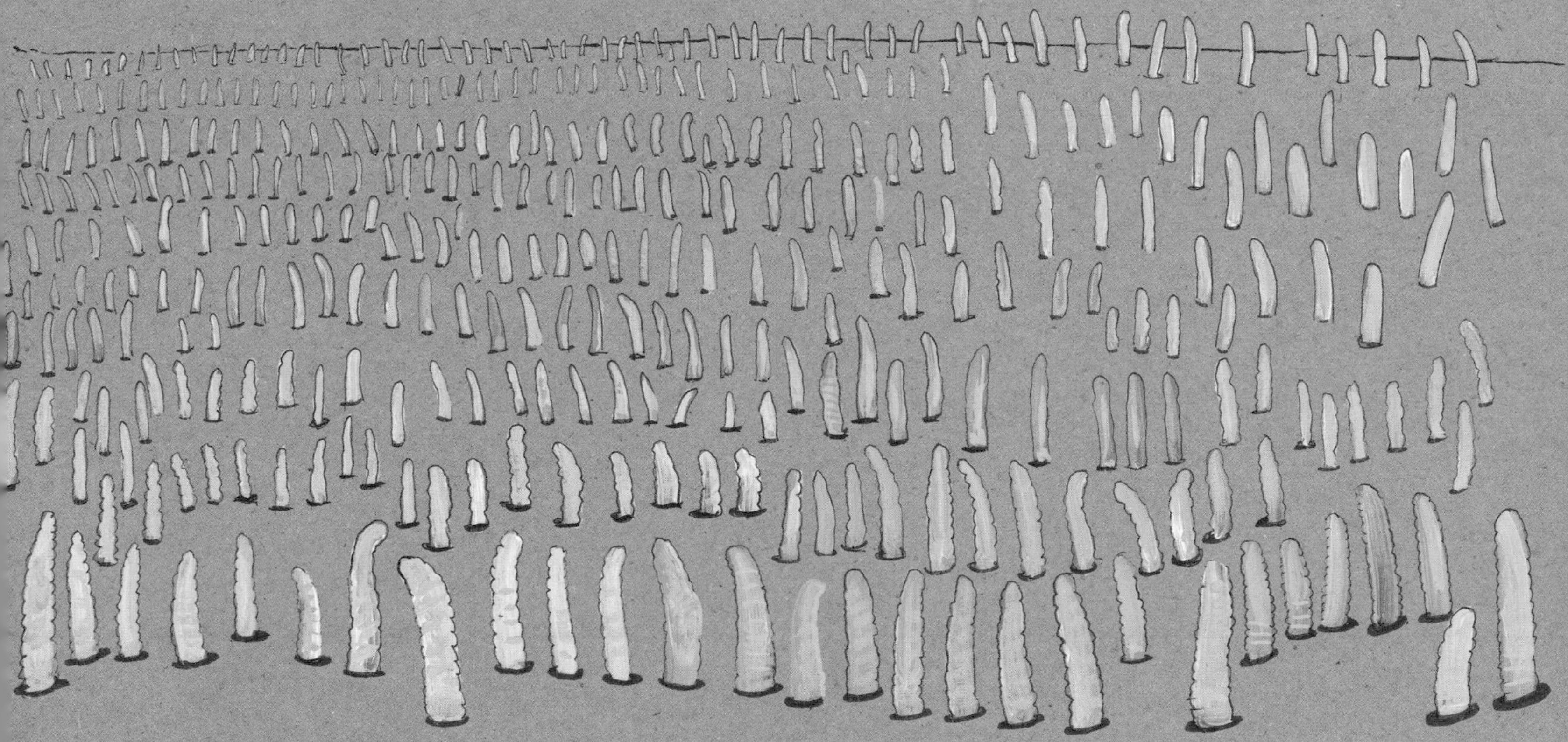

Over ONE MILLION worms can live in a small park.

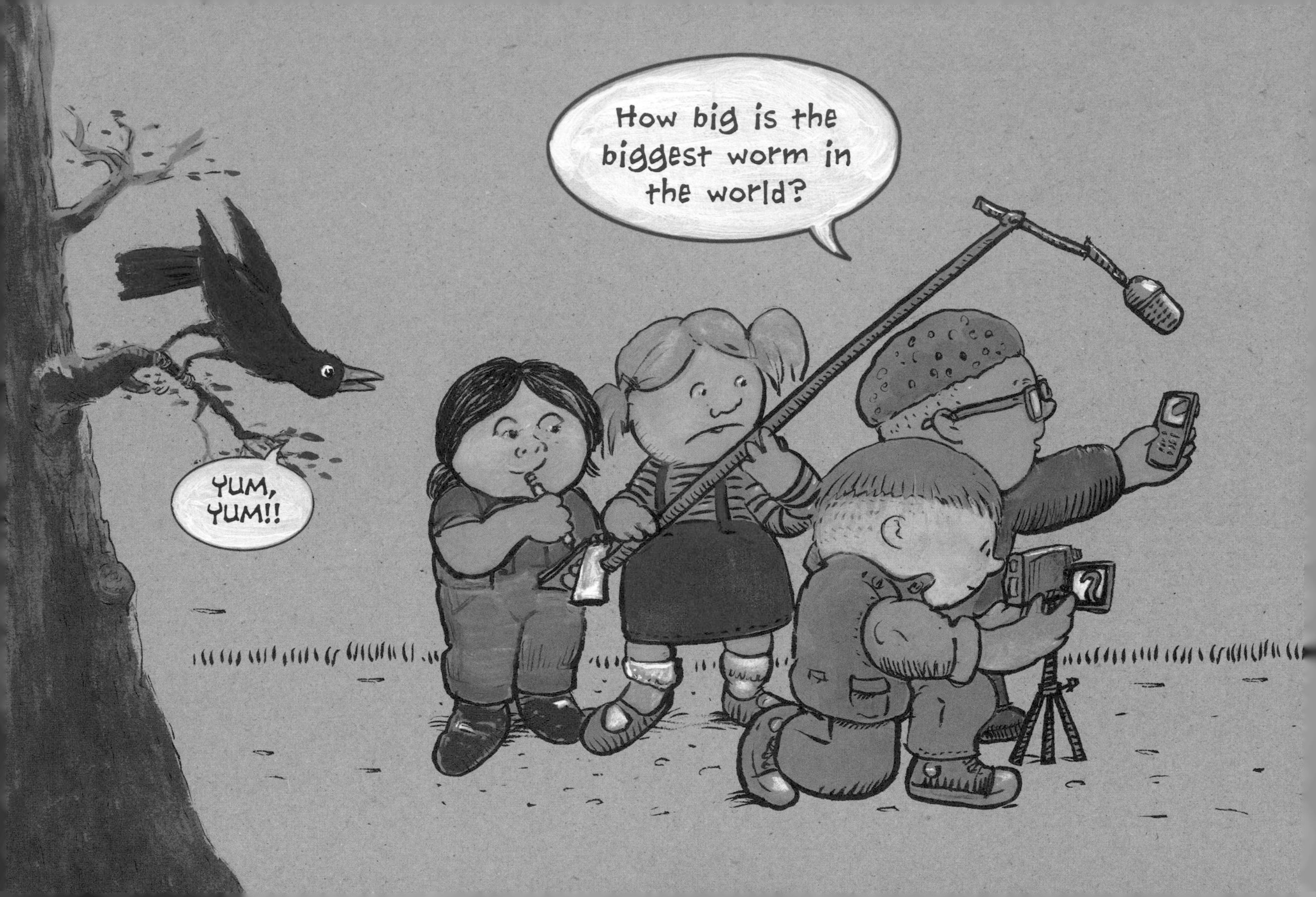
How big is the biggest worm in the world?
YUM, YUM!!

THE AUSTRALIAN GIPPSLAND WORM GROWS TO 10 FEET LONG.

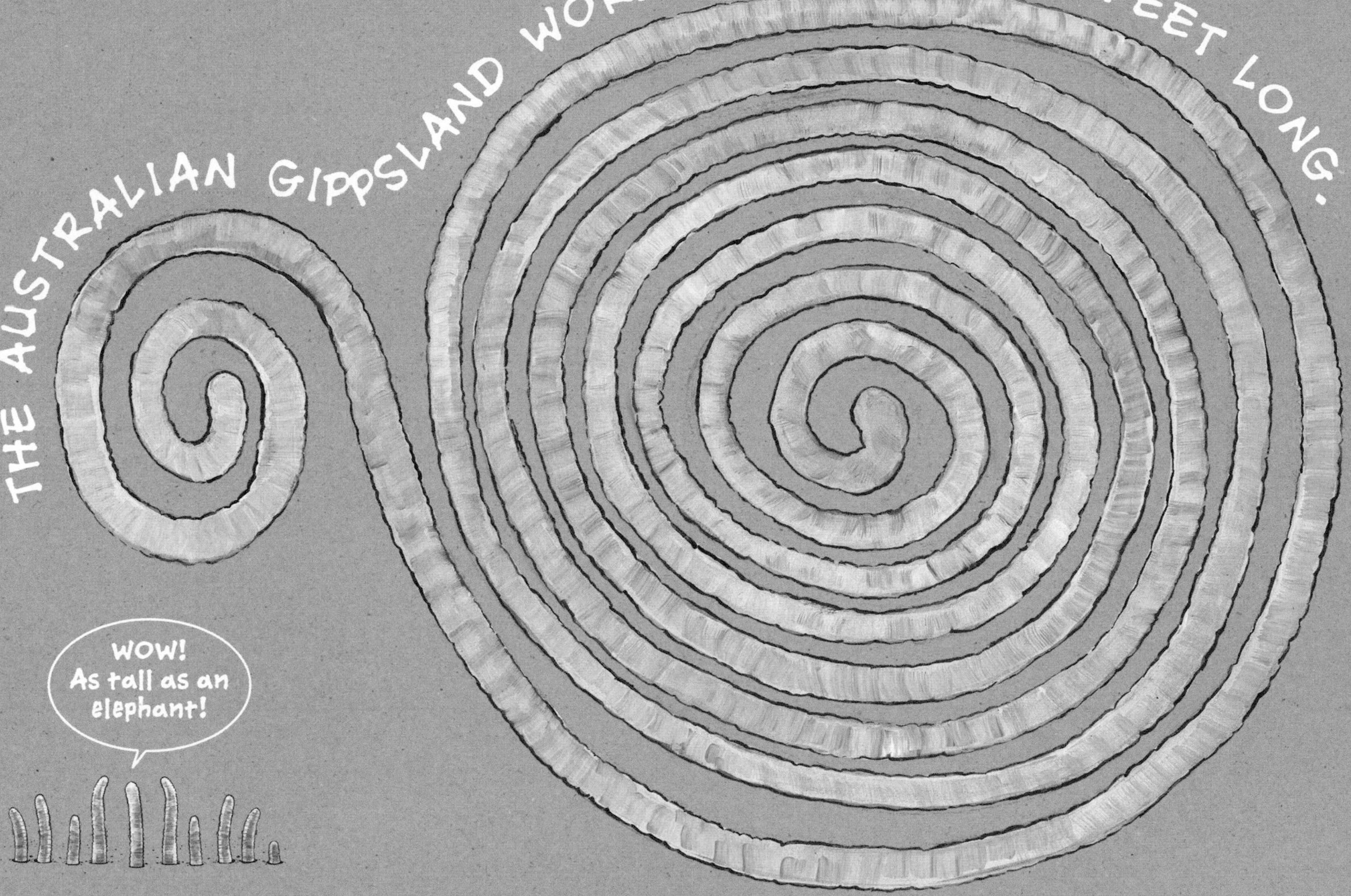
WOW!
As tall as an elephant!

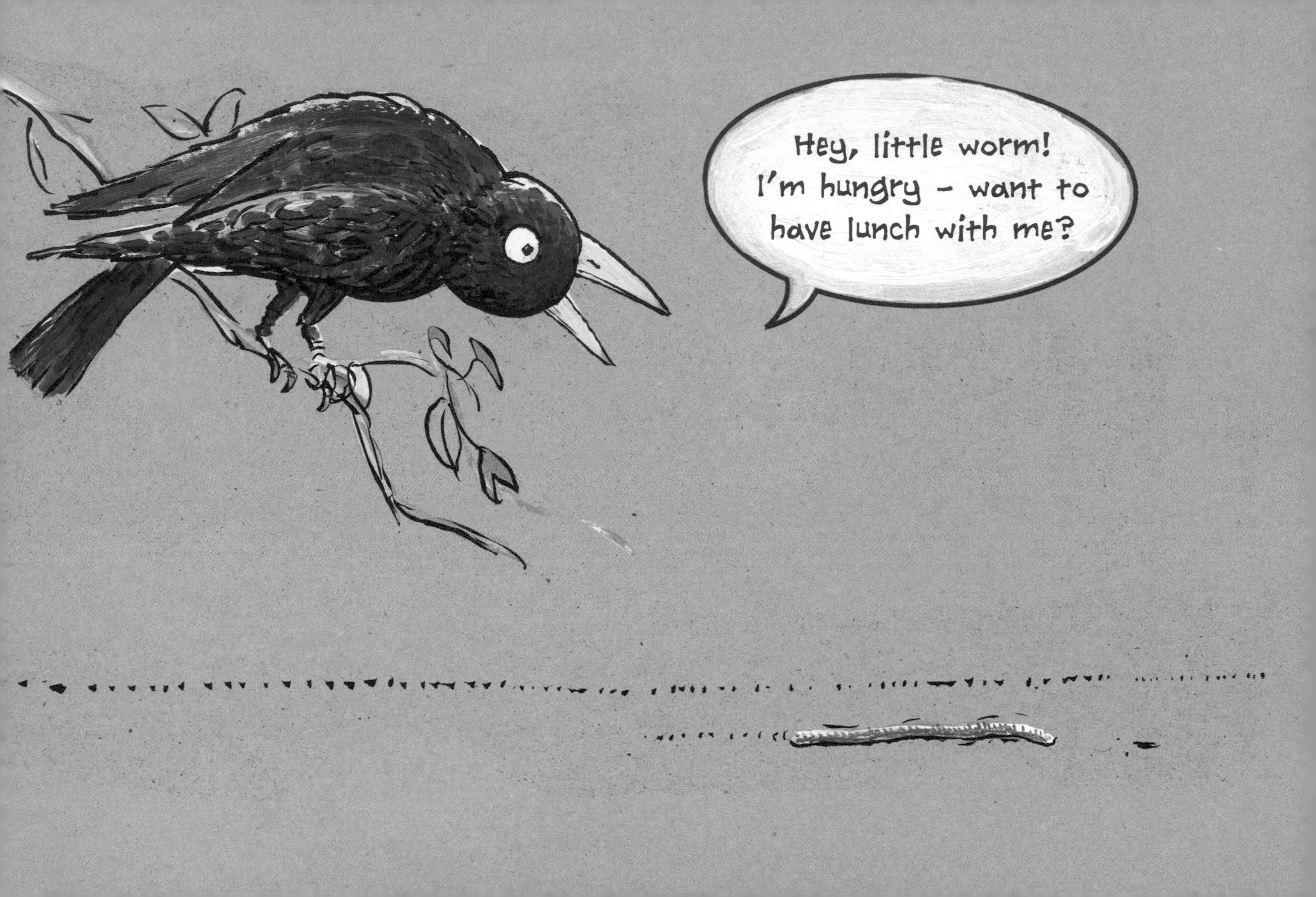
Hey, little worm! I'm hungry - want to have lunch with me?

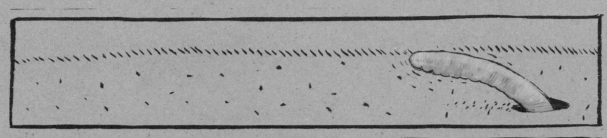

WHY DID THE LITTLE WORM GO AWAY?
WAS IT SOMETHING BLUEBIRD SAID?

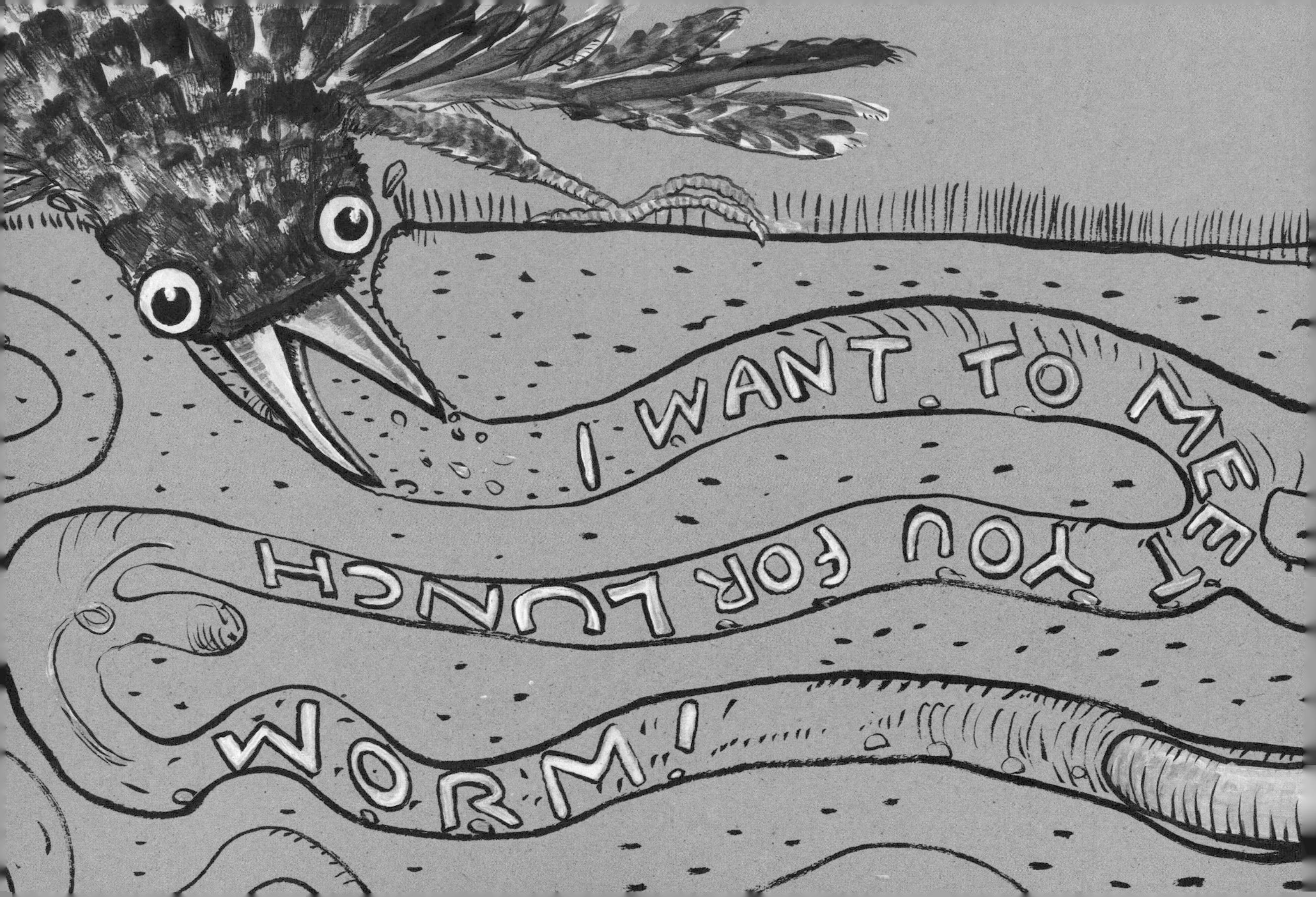
I WANT TO MEET YOU FOR LUNCH
WORM!

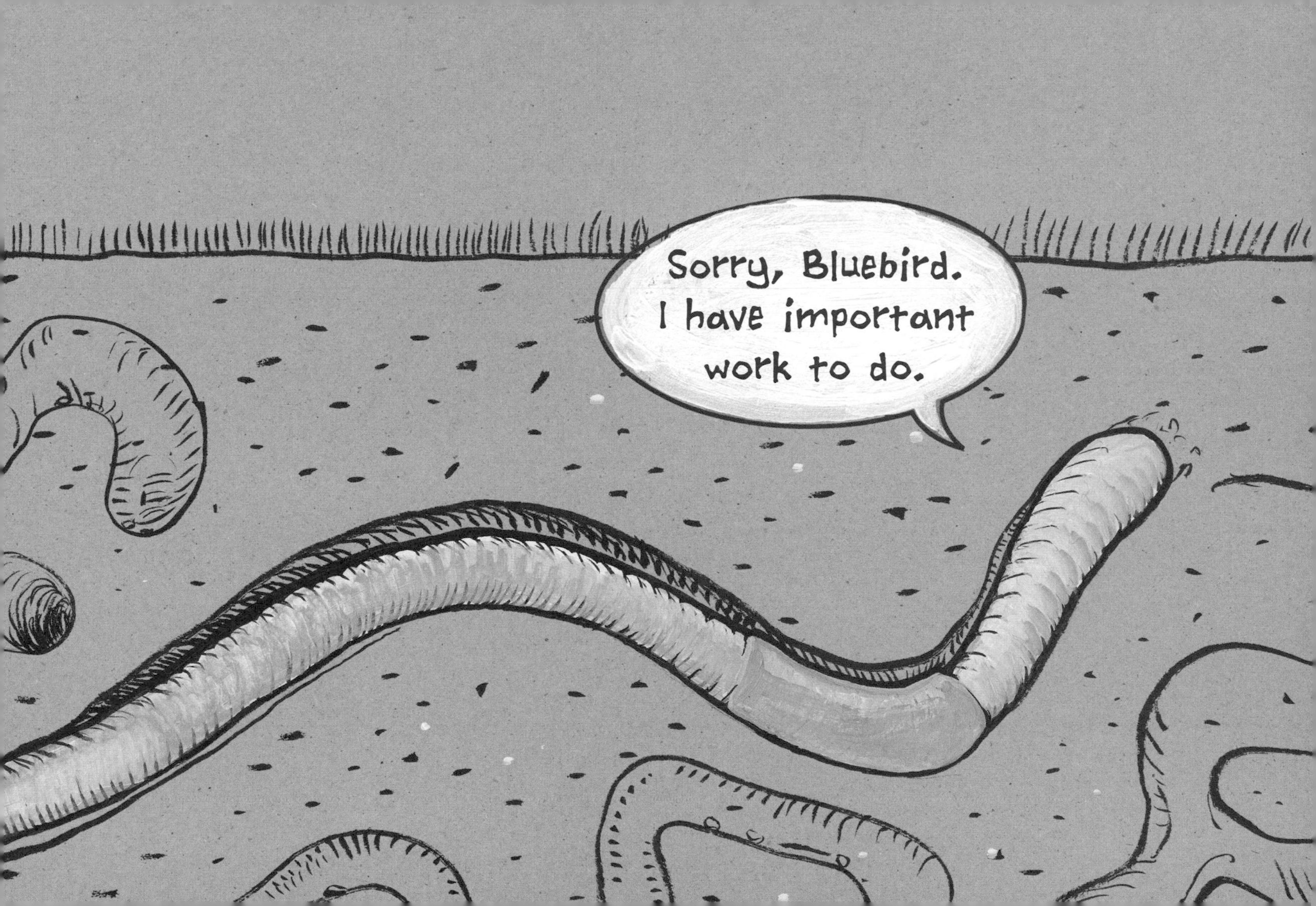
Sorry, Bluebird. I have important work to do.

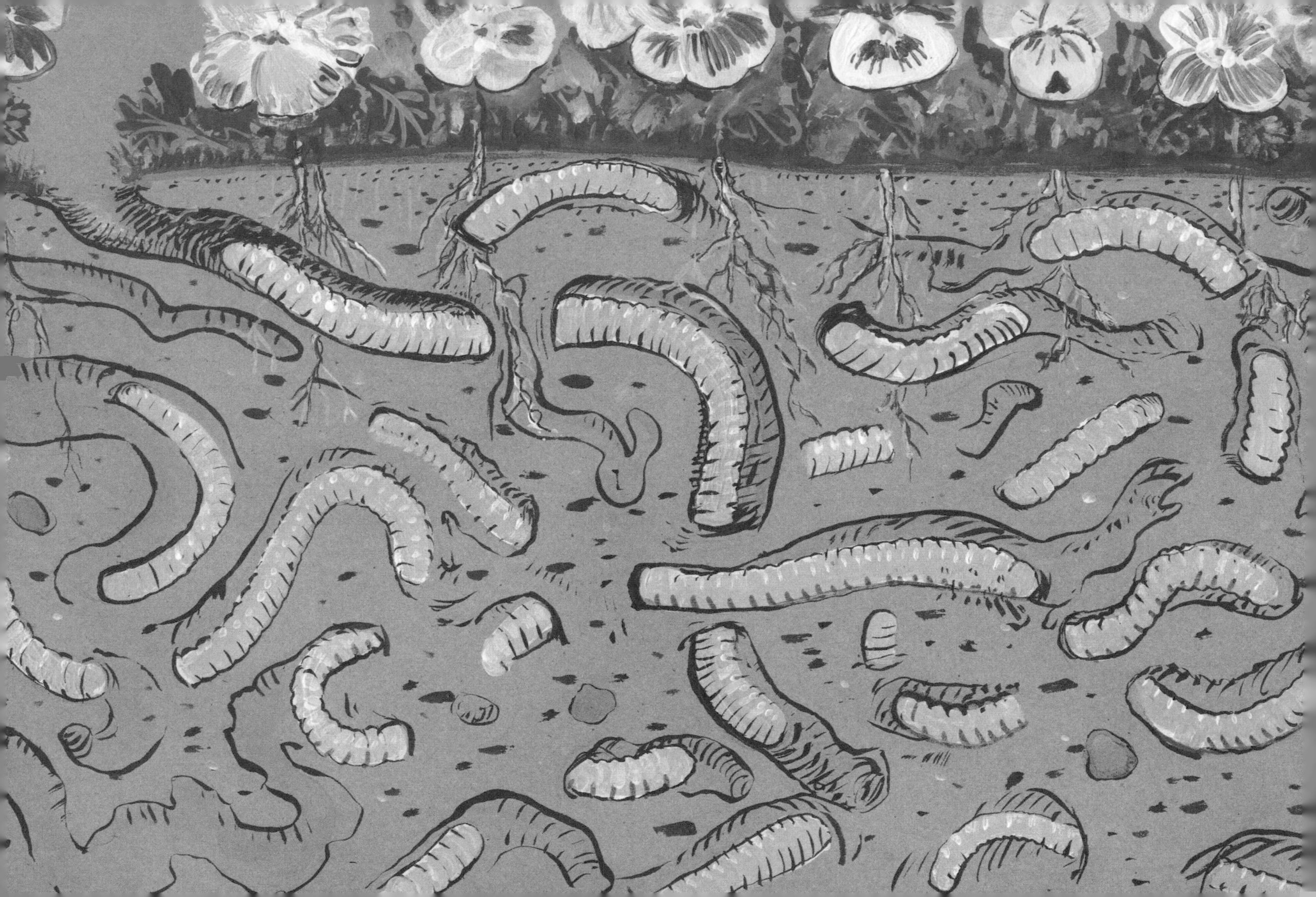

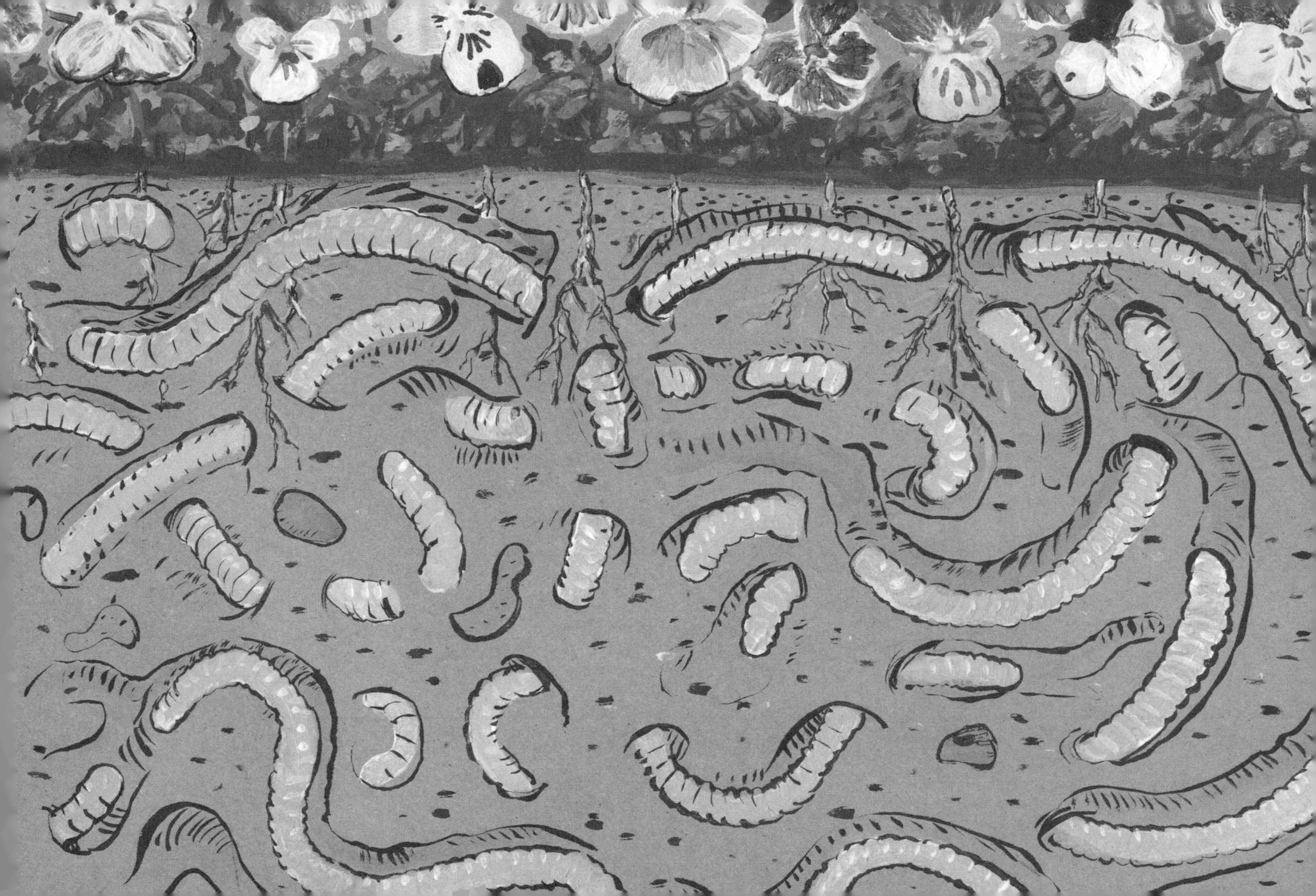

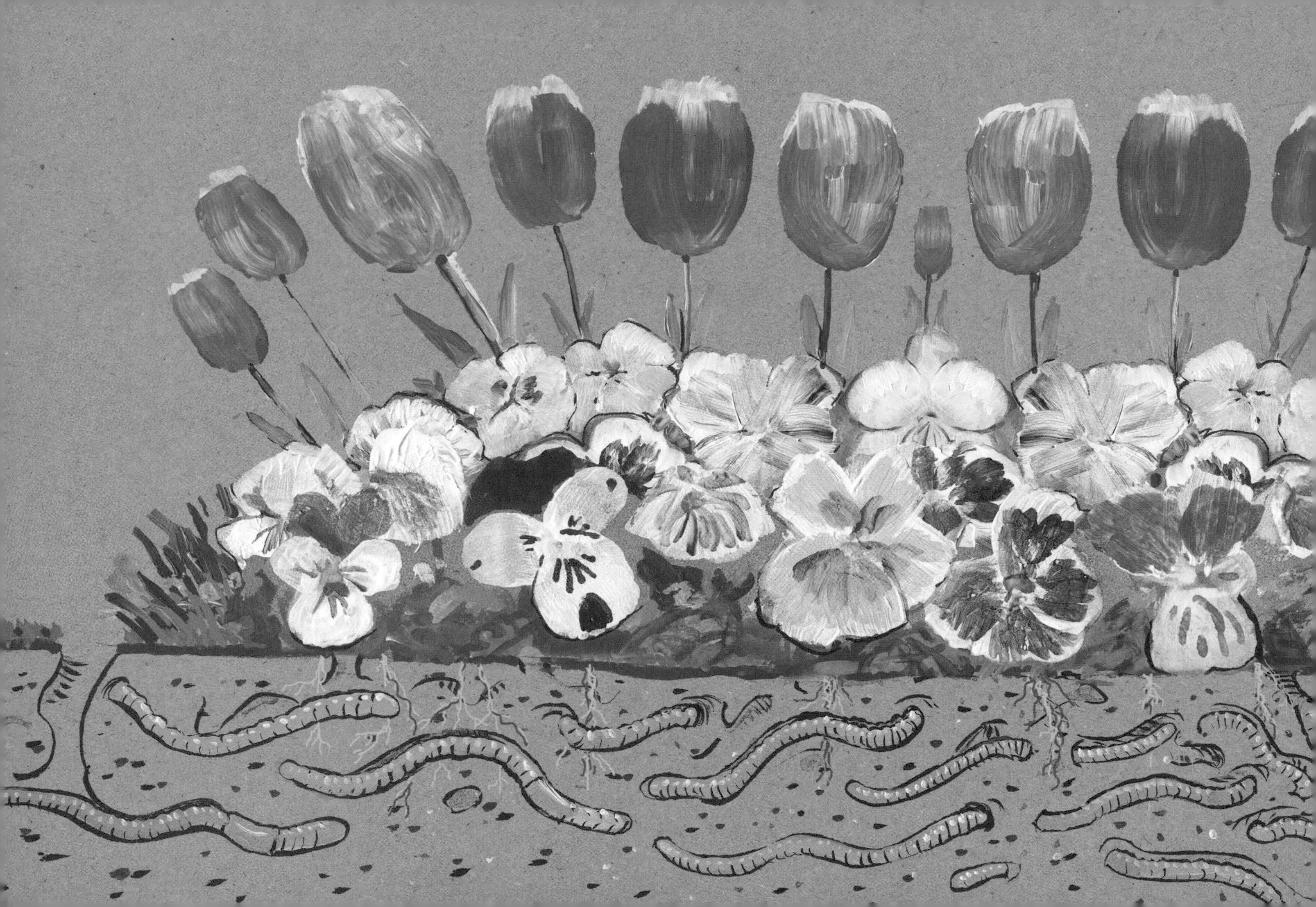

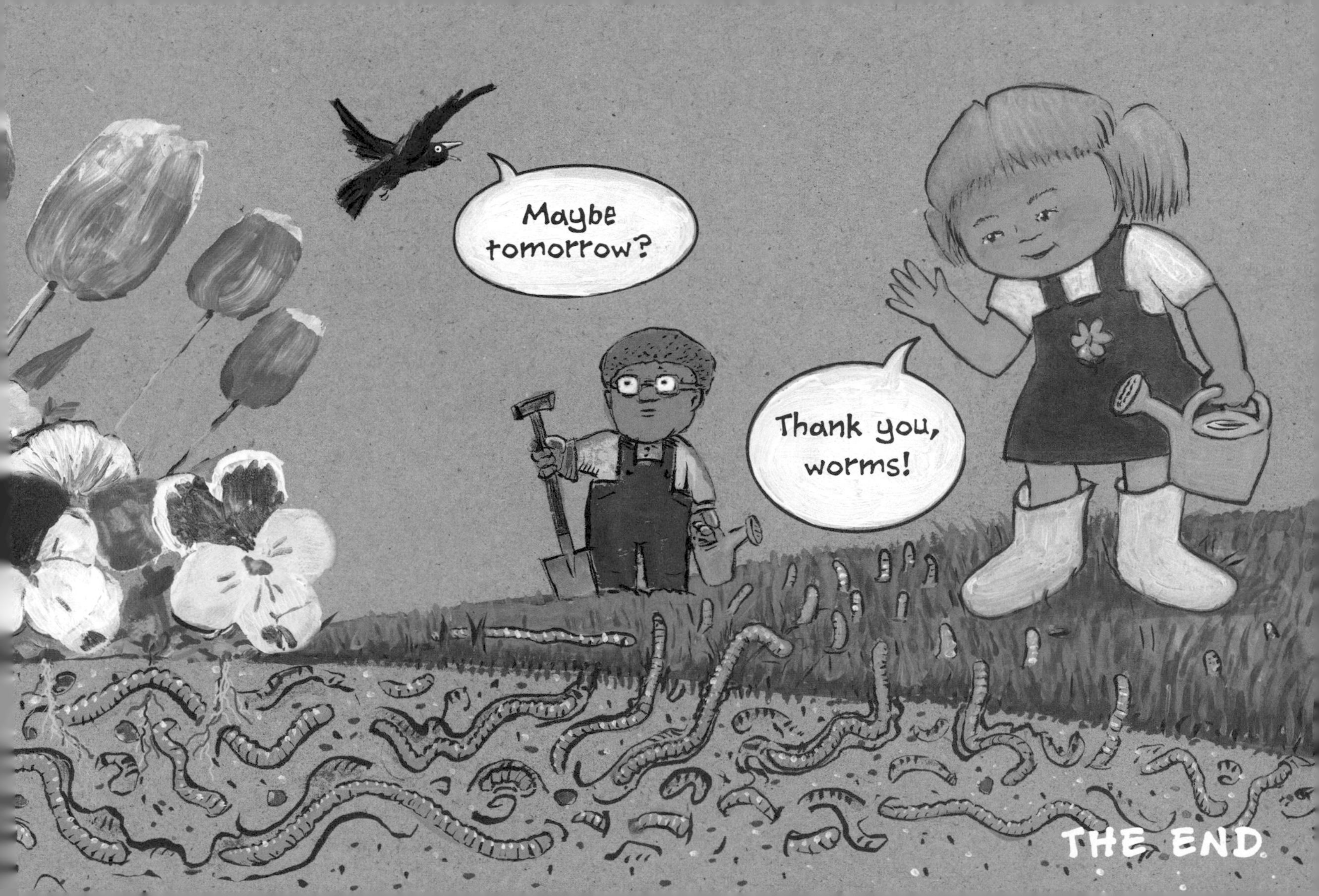
Maybe tomorrow?
Thank you, worms!
THE END

ABOUT THE AUTHOR

Kevin McCloskey teaches illustration at Kutztown University in Pennsylvania. He painted these worm pictures on recycled grocery bags because, just like worms, he believes in recycling.

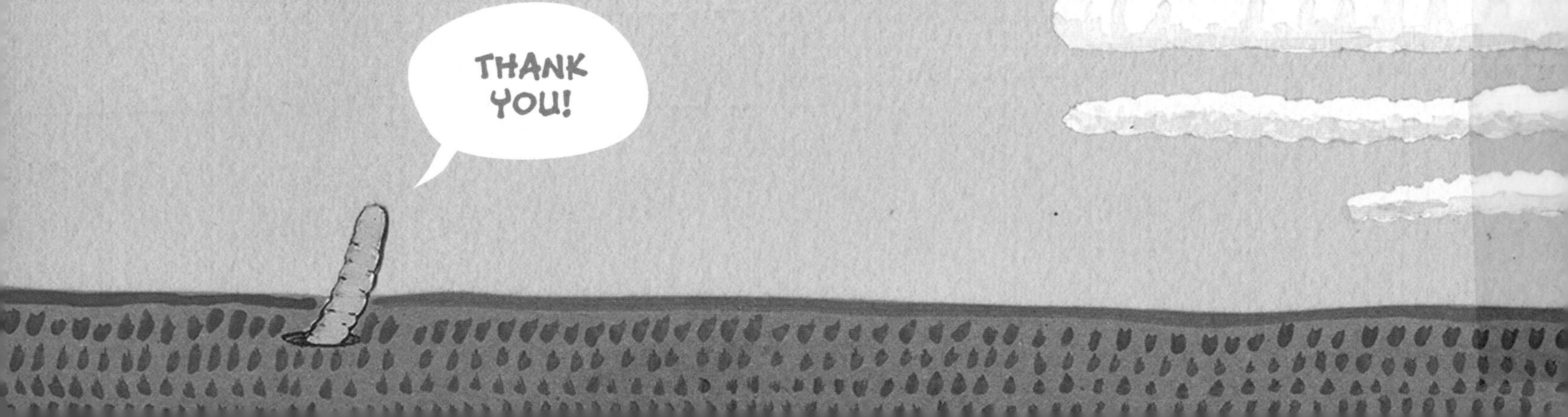
THANK YOU!